Cabin Girl

Cabin Girl

Kristin Butcher

Orca currents

ORCA BOOK PUBLISHERS

Library and Archives Canada Cataloguing in Publication

Butcher, Kristin, author
Cabin girl / Kristin Butcher.
(Orca currents)

Issued in print and electronic formats.
ISBN 978-1-4598-0650-4 (bound).—ISBN 978-1-4598-0649-8 (pbk.).—
ISBN 978-1-4598-0651-1 (pdf).—ISBN 978-1-4598-0652-8 (epub)

I. Title. II. Series: Orca currents
PS8553.U6972C32 2014   jc813'.54   c2013-906740-x
c2013-906741-8

First published in the United States, 2014
Library of Congress Control Number: 2013954153

Summary: At her first job, Bailey learns about workplace bullying.

*Orca Book Publishers is dedicated to preserving the environment and has
printed this book on Forest Stewardship Council® certified paper.*

Orca Book Publishers gratefully acknowledges the support for its
publishing programs provided by the following agencies: the Government
of Canada through the Canada Book Fund and the Canada Council for the Arts,
and the Province of British Columbia through the BC Arts Council
and the Book Publishing Tax Credit.

Cover photography by Getty Images
Author photo by Lisa Pederson Photography

ORCA BOOK PUBLISHERS
PO Box 5626, Stn. B
Victoria, BC Canada
V8R 6S4

ORCA BOOK PUBLISHERS
PO Box 468
Custer, WA USA
98240-0468

www.orcabook.com
Printed and bound in Canada.

17 16 15 14 • 4 3 2 1

For Alan and Helen,
with thanks.

Chapter One

Flying in a Beaver floatplane is like being deaf—only louder. Mrs. Watkins and I don't even try to talk over the engine noise. We peer through our port-holes at Mother Nature's crazy quilt of sun-soaked lakes stitched with forest. The plane is so low, I can see its shadow on the water.

I have butterflies in my stomach. Not because of flying. I've flown dozens of times. I've even flown to Witch Lake but always as a guest. This time I'm going as an employee—thanks to my godfather, Gabe Rutherford. He owns Witch Lake Lodge, and when he offered me a summer job as cabin girl, I jumped at it. I'm going to be cleaning toilets, changing beds and mopping floors. It's not exactly glamorous, but I don't care. I'll be making money. Even better, my parents won't be there. Freedom, at last!

Jim, the pilot, nudges Mr. Watkins and points out the cockpit window. I crane my neck, but the nose of the plane is so high, all I see is blue sky. As if reading my thoughts, Jim lowers one wing and banks left. And there it is—Witch Lake.

It looks different from the air. The first thing I notice is the red-roofed lodge perched on a hill. A deck dotted with yellow umbrellas stretches its entire length. It looks like a giant flower box. The guest cabins are arranged in a tidy semicircle behind the lodge, their paths connecting to the main building like spokes of a wheel. Outbuildings are scattered in out-of-the way corners. Staff quarters line an isolated path leading into the bush. A wide gravel walkway and lush green lawn roll down the hill from the lodge to the lake. It's the middle of the day, which means guests and guides are out fishing, leaving the dock abandoned except for a couple of boats tied to one side. Parked nearby is a trailer hooked to an ATV. Two men are leaning against it. They shield their eyes and look up. One of them is Gabe. I smile and wave, but he doesn't see.

By the time the Beaver taxis in, the place is hopping. The trailer has been backed onto the dock. And two young women, another guy and a big black Lab have shown up. Even before the plane comes to a full stop, Jim jumps out and helps Gabe secure it. The Lab—white-muzzled and heavy with age—wags himself over to Jim. He sniffs the pilot's pants pocket and pushes his nose into his hand. When Jim ignores him, the Lab lifts his head and barks.

Jim laughs and scratches behind the dog's ears. "Can't fool you, can I, old man? Here you go." He reaches into his pocket and offers the dog a treat. Then he scratches the Lab's head again and croons, "Good boy, Sid."

Gabe helps Mrs. Watkins out of the plane, and I jump down behind her. Gabe smiles. "Good to see you, Bailey. It's gonna get busy around here real quick. I hope you're ready."

Without waiting for me to reply, he gestures to the two women standing near the end of the dock. They hurry over. Close up, I see they are younger than I had first thought, probably no more than a few years older than I am. One is tall, blond and athletic looking. The other is tiny, dark and very tanned, which makes the scar zigzagging down her cheek and neck look like white lightning.

"This is Meira and April," Gabe says. "They're our waitresses. They'll introduce you to the other staff and help you get a feel for the place."

I smile shyly. The waitresses do the same.

"April," Gabe says to the one with the scar, "Bailey is going to be your new cabin mate. I'd like you to help her get settled in." Then he turns to Meira. "Let Cook know that Mr. and Mrs. Watkins plan to fish this afternoon, but they need lunch first." He calls to the older man he was standing with earlier. "Ed, tell Josh to get his boat ready. Drake," he hollers to the guy loading luggage onto the trailer, "after you take those bags to cabin four, come back and pick up supplies for the kitchen." He touches my arm and smiles. "Sorry for the rushed welcome, but that's how it is around here. I'll talk to you later." The next thing I know, he's walking the new guests up to the lodge. I get that he's busy, but it doesn't stop me from feeling abandoned.

Within seconds the dock is empty except for April and me—and Jim, who's unloading boxes from the plane. Even the dog has wandered off.

"Come on," April says. "Get your stuff and follow me."

I heave my bulging backpack onto my shoulder and grab the handle of my suitcase. It limps over the boards of the dock like a train on a rickety track. *Clickety, clickety, clickety.* I breathe a relieved sigh when it finally rolls onto the gravel path. Even though it's tougher to pull now, it's quieter.

"Hey, wait up!" I yell to April, who is already way ahead and marching like she's in some kind of walking race.

She stops, turns and shakes her head. "You're going to have to move faster than that if you're going to last around here," she says when I catch up.

"How about you carry the backpack and haul the suitcase and let's see how fast you move?" I retort.

To my surprise, April smiles. "Sorry. I'm used to doing everything in a hurry. It can get pretty hectic around here. If you're not in shape now, you will be soon. Here, gimme your backpack." It's practically as big as she is, but she tosses it onto her shoulder like it's filled with feathers and points toward the bush. "Our cabin is just up that trail."

It's only a three-minute walk, but after fighting with my suitcase the whole way, I'm exhausted. Even so, when I spy a penny in the grass, I bend down to get it.

"What's that?" April says.

I hold up the coin. "See a penny, pick it up, and all day long you'll have good luck."

She rolls her eyes. "You actually believe that?"

I shrug. "It can't hurt." I kiss the coin, shove it into my pocket and follow April inside. She gives me the thirty-second tour.

The cabin is one big room, two if you count the bathroom. Though it's a log structure, its interior is drywall and the floor is tile. There are the usual bedroom furnishings, a few attic-reject paintings and a small table with a couple of mismatched chairs. And that's it for decor.

"So what do you think?" she says.

"Well, I don't see any spiders or cockroaches. That's good."

April flops onto her bed. "And you won't either. I like things clean. I hope you do too. Otherwise you can move into the guides' bunkhouse right now." She closes her eyes and shudders. "Guys are gross."

"Hey, I'm tidy," I tell her. "My mother is a neat freak. If I ever left my room without making my bed, she'd cut me out of the will."

April laughs. "You still live with your parents?"

I nod.

"How old are you?"

"Sixteen. How old are you?"

"Nineteen."

"I gather you don't live with your parents?"

"No way." She snorts. "I don't even know where they are. I've been on my own since I was fourteen."

I feel my eyes widen. "Seriously? Like totally on your own?"

"Pretty much."

I don't know whether to be horrified or impressed. I like the idea of spending the summer away from home, but I can't imagine being on my own full-time.

April walks over to the mirror and starts brushing her hair. As she sweeps it from her face, my eyes are drawn to her scar. I don't want to stare, but I can't help it. I catch her watching me in the mirror and turn away self-consciously.

"Sorry," I mumble.

"No worries," she says. "I'm used to people looking at my scar."

"How'd you get it?" I know it's none of my business, but I blurt the question anyway.

"Motorcycle accident last year. I was in a coma for a couple of days. I got a ruptured spleen, some broken bones—I now have a pin in my hip, and this scar."

"Oh my god, that's awful!" I say.

She shrugs. "It could've been worse."

"How?"

"The guy I was riding with got a funeral."

Chapter Two

Until a few days ago, I thought the worst
sound in the world was the dentist's
drill. My scalp starts to prickle as
soon as I hear that high-pitched whine.
But since I've been working at the lodge,
the drill is a lullaby compared to my
alarm clock. It's the kind you wind up.
Instead of being coaxed awake by music,

I'm jarred awake by clanging. At five thirty in the morning. Every. Single. Day.

I chuck the clock across the room. It crashes into the wall and clatters to the floor but goes right on jangling. I bury my head under the pillow. Finally it stops.

That's when I become aware of another sound. The shower. I peer out from my pillow toward April's side of the room. Her bed is already made. The shower stops, and I know that in a few minutes she'll emerge from the bathroom all smiles and sunshine. I hide under my pillow again. I hate mornings.

My little red wagon grumbles along the gravel path behind me. I don't think it likes mornings either. But apparently fishermen do. Why they have to be on the water so early is a mystery to me.

The fish probably aren't even awake yet. Breakfast is served in the dining room at seven, so it's my job to coax the guests into life at six thirty with coffee and warm muffins delivered to their doors.

Pa-dumpf. I look behind me. One of the baskets of muffins has toppled off the wagon.

Oh, yay. The morning is off to another wonderful start. In the five days I've been at Witch Lake, it's been one disaster after another. I've managed to break three cups, dump a huge container of glass cleaner, spill bleach on a stack of blankets and lose the key to the storage shed. I even accidentally locked Sid in one of the cabins. The poor dog was there all day. I felt really bad about that. And yesterday, my wagon hit a rut and tipped over, throwing its entire cargo of clean sheets into a puddle. Winnie, the laundry lady—who is also my boss—was not impressed.

I push the damaged muffins to one side of the wagon and continue with my deliveries. When I'm done, I head back to the kitchen. Up ahead I see Sid. He's on course to walk straight across the path in front of me. Before that happens, I call him over. He might not be a cat, but he is black, and with the luck I've been having, I don't want to take any chances. Sid immediately changes direction and trots toward me. Disaster averted. I offer him a piece of muffin.

Once the guests hit the lake, I can begin cleaning. In the meantime, I have a half hour to grab some breakfast.

The staff dining room opens onto the back deck of the lodge. The guides have already eaten, so the place is deserted—except for Winnie. Winnie is the grouchiest person I've ever met. She could out-sour lemons! She is always on my case. Even though I haven't done anything wrong yet today—she doesn't know about the muffins—I want to turn around and walk back outside. But I know she's seen me, so I say good morning and head over to the food counter.

I lift the lids of the metal warming pans—cold scrambled eggs, cold bacon, cold pan fries and limp toast. I opt for cereal and juice.

"Six guests out today and eight new ones in, all by ten thirty," Winnie says before I even sit down. "So cabins three, eight and nine get a change of linen as well as a cleaning. And you'll need to wash the floors in all the cabins. With yesterday's rain, there will be mud everywhere. When you're done with that, you can help me hang bedding on the line to air."

I pour milk on my cereal and nod. Winnie slurps her coffee. When the screen door opens, we both look up.

"Morning, ladies." Ed smiles, and his eyes crinkle at the corners. He grabs a mug. "How's the coffee?"

"Wet," Winnie says. I'm amazed at how grumpy she can sound with one word.

"Just how I like it." Ed smiles again and picks up the carafe. "Can I pour you another cup, Winnie?"

She shakes her head and sets her cup in the dirty-dish bin. "I have work to do." Then she taps her watch and glares at me. "And so do you. Best get to it."

"Yes, Winnie," I mumble and start to get up.

Ed puts a hand on my shoulder. "Let the girl finish her breakfast, Winnie. The guests haven't even left the dining room yet."

Winnie doesn't answer. She just scowls and stomps out the door.

I don't get it. The woman is in a perpetual bad mood. Someone needs to give her smiling lessons. I glance at Ed. He would be the guy for the job. He has happy lines even when he's not smiling.

"She hates me," I say when the screen door bangs shut.

Ed takes the seat Winnie vacated and, of course, smiles. "That's just her way. Don't take it personal."

"But I do! It's like she's waiting for me to screw up. She's such a—" I stop before I say something I might regret.

Ed looks at me over the top of his mug. "Such a…?"

I shake my head. "Let's just say she's working at the right place."

Ed's eyebrows dive together in a puzzled frown.

I lean toward him and whisper, "Witch Lake. I think the place was named after her."

Ed says, "I wouldn't let Winnie hear you say that."

We both smile. Then Ed returns to his coffee, and I finish my cereal.

As I push the bowl away, I ask, "How did the lake get its name?"

He gets up and pours more coffee. "There's a legend," he says, "about a fur trader who lived on the lake back in the seventeen hundreds. Like most trappers, he was a loner. He spent the winter months here in northern Manitoba. Then, in the spring, he'd head south and sell his furs.

"He married himself a Cree woman, the daughter of a shaman. After a time, they had a little girl, built a cabin and settled on the lake. But every spring he'd leave for a few weeks to trade his furs.

"One afternoon while he was away, three woodsmen stumbled upon the cabin. Seeing the place was occupied, they hid behind some trees and watched all afternoon and into the evening. The moon was full, so it was easy to see. When they were sure the woman and her teenage daughter were alone, they moved in and took the cabin by force.

"Mother and daughter fought hard, but they were outnumbered and over-powered. During the skirmish, the mother was thrown against a wall. Her neck snapped, and she died instantly."

I gasp. "Oh, no! That's terrible! What about the girl?"

Ed takes a gulp of coffee before he continues. "That's the crazy part. According to the legend, she went into a trance and started chanting in Cree. Then—right there in the cabin—she turned into a giant black bear. In a matter of minutes, she tore two of the woodsmen to pieces. Then she burst into flame, burning the cabin to the ground. The last woodsman raced back to civilization.

"Of course, when he told people what had happened, nobody believed him. They thought he'd lost his mind, which, by that time, he pretty much had."

"What about the fur trader?"

"He went back to the lake, but there was nothing there—no cabin and no sign of his wife or daughter."

"Not even ashes or bones?"

Ed shakes his head. "All he found was his daughter's necklace. It was on the ground at the edge of the lake. The necklace had been passed down through the shaman's family and was thought to be magical. The girl had never taken it off. Legend has it that every full moon, she comes back to the lake to look for it."

A shiver races up my spine. "You mean her ghost?"

He nods. "That's what they say. Some of the guests at the lodge have claimed they've seen her."

Kristin Butcher

I feel the blood drain out of me.
"Have you?"

Ed pushes back his chair and stands
up. "Not so far." For once, he's not
smiling.

Chapter Three

Somehow I make it through my first two weeks at the lodge without getting fired. It could be because Gabe is never around when I mess up, which is amazing, since I mess up a lot. The harder I try to do things right, the more goes wrong. Thank goodness for April. If it wasn't for our nighttime chats, I'd probably crawl under a rock and never come out. But she understands what I'm going through.

We are getting ready for bed after a long day when I admit how much I hate being the butt of everyone's jokes. I feel sick about my mistakes, but everybody else in camp acts like they're a big joke. You'd think I'd been hired as comic relief instead of a cabin girl.

"It's like that for everyone at the beginning," she says. "Don't worry about it."

I sigh. "You don't understand. This was supposed to be my chance to show everyone that I'm not a little kid anymore."

"Show who?"

I shrug. "My parents mostly. I'm sixteen years old, but they treat me like I'm ten. I have to get their approval for every little thing I do. For instance, all my friends are getting their drivers' licenses, but not me. Even though the law says I'm old enough, my parents think I'm too young. If I do okay here, I'm hoping they'll let me make my own decisions." I roll my eyes. "The only reason they let me take this job is because Gabe owns the camp, and even then I had to beg to be allowed to do it. They're counting on Gabe to keep an eye on me. Like he has the time. He's so busy he barely knows I'm here."

April laughs. "That's good, right?"

I smile sheepishly. "I guess." Then I add quietly, "I wish I was like you."

"What d'ya mean?"

"You know—independent, the boss of myself. I want to run my own life— like you do. No one tells you what to do. You can do anything you want."

"I don't know about that, but I do like trying new things. Like, when the season is over here at the lodge, I'm going to—"

Suddenly April stops talking.

"What?" I say. "What are you going to do?"

She shakes her head. "Nothing. I shouldn't have said anything. It's not for sure yet."

"Come on, April. Tell me. I won't say anything." When she doesn't answer, I add, "Hey, I shared my secret with you."

For another minute or so, April looks at me like she's trying to decide. Finally, she says, "Okay, but you can't tell anybody. Promise?"

I nod and cross my heart. "Absolutely."

"Okay," she says again and leans in closer. "I'm going to open a flower shop. Come the fall, I should have enough money saved."

"April, that's great! You see? I was right. You can do anything."

It's been three whole days without a screwup, so I think I'm over whatever my problem was. Now that I know what I'm doing, I'm more relaxed. I'm not tired all the time either, and I don't ache everywhere. Lately I've even been waking up before the alarm, though that might only be self-defense.

Best of all, I'm starting to fit in with camp life. Everyone is really friendly. Well, everyone except Winnie. But I think Ed's right about her. She's just naturally grumpy.

Today was a great day. I got a tip from some guests, so after supper I decide to buy myself a treat at the camp store. The Witch's Lair, as it's called, is open in the morning before the guests go fishing and then again for a couple of hours in the evening. There's not a lot in it—mostly fishing gear, chocolate bars, sunglasses, mosquito repellent, that sort of thing. Drake usually runs the store, but this evening Ed is behind the counter.

"Well, look who the wind blew in," he says with a wink. "What can I get for you, Bailey?"

"Ice cream. I've been dreaming about it all day."

He gestures to the freezer. "Help yourself."

I lift the lid and start digging around inside. When somebody jabs me in the ribs, I look up. It's April. She's come for cigarettes. Like most everyone in camp, she smokes.

"Ice cream's better," I holler as she leaves.

She turns and gives me the finger, but she's smiling, so I grin back.

"You two getting along all right?" Ed asks when she's gone.

I nod. "For sure. April's great— kinda like my Witch Lake Lodge big sister. Well, maybe not big—she's pretty little, but you know what I mean."

"I never had a sister."

"Me neither. But if I did, I'd want her to be like April."

"Why's that?"

I shrug. "She's smart. She's good at her job, and she's tough. Did you know she's been on her own since she was fourteen?"

"Nope. Can't say that I did."

"Well, she has. And as you can see, she's doing fine." I want to tell Ed how April's going to open a flower shop, but I promised April I'd keep that information to myself, so I don't say anything.

Ed pulls back and squints at me. "Are you the president of her fan club or what?"

I frown. "Now you're making fun of me."

He shakes his head. "Sorry. I don't mean to. You're actually a breath of fresh air around here. So I'd hate—"

April pokes her head back in the open doorway. "Come on, Bailey."

She gestures for me to hurry. "The guys have set up the volleyball net. We're going to have a game." Then her head disappears again.

"Well, what are you waiting for?" Ed says. "Get out there."

After the game, one of the guides walks April and me back to our cabin. His name is Sloan, and he's totally hot. His abs ripple right through his T-shirt. But he's a lot older than I am. If Gabe even suspected I liked him, I'd be on the next plane home. Besides, Sloan has a thing for April. I can tell. I think she likes him too.

I glance up at the moon. It's lopsided, like somebody shaved away part of one side. In a few more days, it will be full. The thought makes my heart skip a few beats.

"Do you guys know anything about the Witch Lake legend?" I ask.

"Sure," Sloan says. "Everybody knows the legend. Why?"

I heave a sigh. "No reason. It's just such a sad story, and it's kind of spooky. Ed says the witch comes back to look for her necklace when the moon is full." I point to the sky. "That's pretty soon."

April laughs. "Don't tell me you buy all that mumbo jumbo. It's just a story. We tell it to the guests to make the lake seem mysterious." She laughs again.

"But it has to be true," I argue.

"Why?"

"Because Ed said some of the guests have seen her."

"No doubt." Sloan chuckles. "After a few drinks, people see all kinds of things."

He and April laugh again and go back to flirting. When we get to the cabin, I leave them on the steps and get ready for bed. I'm under the covers and flipping through a magazine when April comes in. I expect her to start gushing about Sloan, but all she does is grab a hand mirror and tweezers off her bureau, plunk herself on her bed and start working on her eyebrows. When she's done, she puts the mirror and tweezers down and heads into the bathroom.

There's clearly not going to be any girl talk tonight, so I toss the magazine onto the night table, switch out the light and burrow beneath my covers. Right away I start to drift off. There's nothing like fresh air and exercise to conk a person out. I don't even hear April come back into the room.

Crash!

I bolt upright. "What was that?"

"Sorry," April says. She's on her knees, picking up glass shards. "I broke the mirror. I forgot I left it on the bed, and when I pulled back the covers, it fell on the floor." She pads across the room to get the broom and dustpan.

"That's seven years bad luck," I murmur.

She stops sweeping and blinks at me in disbelief. Finally she shakes her head. "You have to be the most superstitious person I have ever met. On Friday the thirteenth, you stay in bed all day, don't you? The only bad thing about breaking that mirror, Bailey, is that now I have no mirror."

I know April thinks I'm being silly, but I don't back down. "You can call me superstitious if you want," I say. "I call it being careful. Things happen all the time that people can't explain. I'm not saying there are such things as spirits, but you can't prove there aren't."

April closes her eyes and shakes her head. "God, Bailey, get a grip."

"Just do one thing," I say. "Turn around three times, counterclockwise."

"Why? To make the spirits dizzy? Don't be dumb."

"It'll take you two seconds. It might not undo your seven years of bad luck, but it can't hurt."

"You're serious, aren't you?"

I don't say anything.

She closes her eyes again, but she does spin around. "There. Are you happy now?"

I bob my head. "Yup."

Chapter Four

It's a major changeover day at the lodge.
Half the guests are moving out and a
new bunch are moving in. That means
a busy morning for me.

I finish cleaning the cabins and
changing the beds as the first plane
arrives. It's only eleven o'clock, but
the day is already hot, and my T-shirt
is sticking to me. As I pile the last of

the soiled linen into my little red wagon, I glance toward the dock. There are bodies, boxes and bags everywhere. It looks like mass confusion, but it's not. In a few minutes the new guests will be on their way to the lodge, the departing guests will be winging their way home, and the dock will be empty—until the next plane comes in. I grab the handle of my wagon and head for the washhouse. After leaving the dirty laundry with Winnie, I make my way to the storage shed to park my wagon.

My stomach growls. Time for lunch. I've barely started up the path to the staff dining room when I hear my name. I look around to see Gabe standing in front of the lodge, waving me over. One of the new guests is with him.

The man and Gabe are probably around the same age, but Gabe's body is hard and lean while the other guy looks like he's spent his life behind a desk.

He's on the short side, balding and thick through the middle. The parts of him that aren't fleshed out are giving way to gravity. But he has a friendly face, and when Gabe introduces us, the man smiles like he means it.

"Bailey," Gabe says, "this is Dennis Savoy. He'll be with us for the next three days. Cabin two. Dennis, this is Bailey. She's our cabin girl. She'll be knocking on your door with morning coffee and tidying up while you're fishing."

The man sticks out his hand. "Nice to meet you, Bailey."

I don't usually get introduced to guests, so I'm a bit puzzled. I return the guy's handshake. "Welcome to Witch Lake, Mr. Savoy."

"Bailey, I wonder if you could show Mr. Savoy to his cabin to get his tackle box and then take him to the store to pick up some fishing gear. Ed will meet you there."

I nod and smile. "Sure. No problem."

Gabe glances at his watch. "See you back here for lunch at noon, Dennis."

As if on cue, an engine sounds overhead, a plane clears the trees, and Gabe takes off for the dock.

"Busy place," Dennis Savoy says as we start up the path leading to the guest cabins.

I nod. "On changeover days for sure. Otherwise, it's pretty peaceful."

"And beautiful," he adds, lowering the case he's carrying and kneeling to open it.

Inside is an impressive-looking camera, complete with a big zoom lens. He slips the strap around his neck, pops off the lens cap and starts shooting. He swings around one way and then the other like he's on a swivel.

"Are you a photographer?" I ask when he finally lowers the camera.

"Nah," he smiles. "Just a wannabe." He puts the lens cap back on, and we continue walking.

"Is this your first time to Witch Lake?" I ask.

"Actually, it's my first time to any fly-in fishing lodge."

"Really? Well, you made the right choice. You're going to love it here."

"Good to know. Truth is, I didn't choose this place. The fishing trip was arranged for me."

"Sweet." I grin. I noticed a wedding ring on his finger when we shook hands, so I say, "A gift from your wife?"

He shakes his head. "No. The people I work with set it up."

As the guest cabins come into view, he stops and snaps a few more photos. Then he says, "I'm not really much of a fisherman. Oh, I've done some fishing, but nothing like most of the people who come here."

"I kinda figured that," I say.

"Oh?" He looks surprised. "What gave me away?"

I try not to smile. "Well, you're looking to get some gear from the store, for one thing. Most guests come here with enough gear for five people. Also, you're not really dressed for fishing— dress pants, dress shoes, dress shirt…" I shrug and leave the sentence hanging.

He grins. "Hey, I ditched the tie."

We both laugh.

"So did you come straight from work to the plane?"

He pauses. "Sort of."

"What do you do?" And then, because I realize it's none of my business, I back-track. "Sorry. I shouldn't be so nosy."

He waves my apology away. "It's a natural question. Everybody works."

We've reached his cabin, so we put our conversation on pause and I sit down on the step while he goes inside.

When he returns, he has his tackle box and he's changed his clothes. He's wearing cargo pants, a short-sleeved shirt and deck shoes. It's not quite jeans and runners, but it's definitely an improvement.

As he locks the door, I say, "Do you have a hat and sunglasses? Sunscreen? It can get pretty intense on the water."

He shakes his head.

"Never mind. You can get those at the store too."

We begin walking and he chuckles. "Are you sure you're not somebody's mother?"

I snort and shake my head.

"So this is a summer job?" he says.

"Yeah. The lodge is open from mid-May to mid-September, depending on the weather, but I'm only here for July and August. I have school the rest of the time."

He nods. "Are most of the staff high-school kids?"

I shake my head. "No. I'm the only one. Everyone else is older. Some just come for a summer or two to earn money for university. But Cook, Winnie and Ed have been working here for years. For some staff, it fills a gap until they find something more permanent." I grin. "Like April—she's one of the waitresses. When fishing season's over, she's going to open a flower shop." I kind of gasp as I realize I've blabbed April's secret. Not that telling a guest is going to matter.

Dennis Savoy nods. "So how many people work here?"

I shrug. "I've never counted, but a full camp is forty-four guests, so that's twenty-two guides right there. Actually, twenty-three. Gabe likes to keep an extra on hand. Then there's Cook and the kitchen girl, the laundry lady, April and Meira, Tricia, the camp boy, Gabe, Ed and me. I'm the cabin girl."

"That must be tough, cleaning the cabins all by yourself. If you're the only one, how do you get a day off?"

"I don't," I tell him. "Nobody does. Working at the lodge is a twenty-four/seven job. But it's not like we're hard at it all day. After I deliver coffee and clean the cabins, I'm pretty much done. I might dust and vacuum the lodge, and sometimes I help the laundry lady fold bedding, but that's about it. The girls in the kitchen have it harder than me. Cook works all day long."

"And the waitresses?"

"Mostly they serve the meals— breakfast and supper. Lunch too if there are new guests, like today. Basically, they're responsible for the dining room. Setting tables, filling salt and pepper shakers, making sure the bar is stocked and serving food. If it's really busy, they help Cook in the kitchen."

I see Ed standing in the doorway to the store, so I wave. He waves back.

I turn to Dennis Savoy. "Well, Mr. Savoy, this is it. Ed will help you from here. Enjoy your stay."

As I jog toward the staff dining room, I think about Dennis Savoy and the conversation we just had. He seems like a nice guy, and he's certainly easy to talk to. We covered a lot ground of during our little walk. And he took a pile of pictures. The thing that puzzles me, though, is why someone who isn't really interested in fishing would come to a fishing lodge.

Chapter Five

"After you finish serving breakfast, do you want to help me clean cabins?" I ask April as we make our way up to the lodge the next morning. "With two of us, we'd be finished in no time. Then we'd have the entire afternoon to chill. We could paint our nails, flip through fashion magazines and pig out on chocolate. My mom sent me a care package." I waggle my eyebrows.

The frown on April's face tells me she is not impressed. "You want me to clean cabins? Forget it. Been there, done that. I'll stick to waitressing, thanks. The tips are better." Then her face clears. "But I will help you eat that chocolate."

Since there are guests in every cabin and only me to clean them, my morning's work stretches into early afternoon. I start with cabin eleven and work my way backward. It's an easy way to keep track of how many I have left to do. Dennis Savoy's cabin is next to last, so by the time I get to it, I'm feeling punch-drunk tired and light-headed from hunger. It's no wonder I dump the contents of the wastebasket all over the floor.

I growl through gritted teeth as I kneel to scoop the mess into a garbage bag. Thank goodness there aren't any pencil shavings, used tissues or chewed gum in the debris. Mostly, it's crumpled paper, and I have it picked up in a few seconds.

But there's one item that eludes me—a coffee-stained business card that gloms onto the floor like it was glued there. I try to lift a corner. I try to slip a fingertip under the side. I even try pushing on the ends to crumple it. The card stays pasted to the floor. Finally I pull off one of my latex gloves, lick my finger, stab it onto the back of the card and lift. The card rises off the floor for a split second before letting go, but it's long enough.

"Gotcha!" I mutter as I snatch it in midair. Then, as if I need to identify my adversary, I flip it over and read the front. The embossed logo is a bird in flight and the company name, Hawke & Associates. Below that is Dennis Savoy's name and his job title. Then there's a telephone number and email address.

I read the card again. Dennis Savoy is a field investigator. I'm fairly certain he doesn't investigate pastures and meadows, but that's as far as my powers of deduction go. He's an investigator of something, though I have no idea what. And I can't ask him without incriminating myself. The business card was in the wastebasket, so the only way I could possibly have read it is by snooping through his trash. If he found out, he might report me to Gabe. Gabe would probably fire me. And my parents would never let me out of their sight again until I'm thirty.

I have no choice but to put the matter out of my head. That's easier said than done, especially when I exit the cabin and see Dennis Savoy standing beside my wagon. Before I have a chance to hide my surprise, he snaps my photo. Talk about a picture of guilt.

He laughs. "You should see the look on your face."

My guilt morphs into indignation. "Why did you do that?"

He must realize I'm upset, because the smile slides from his mouth, and he apologizes. "Sorry." Then he pushes a couple of buttons on the camera and says, "There. The photo's gone."

I'm still a bit shaken, but I make myself smile. After all, Dennis Savoy is a guest. As I pile everything into my wagon and prepare to move to the last cabin, I try to sound cheerful. "How was fishing?"

"Great. My guide really knows his stuff."

I glance at my watch. "You're back early."

He sighs. "Yeah. I'm beat. Too much sun, I think."

"Can I get you anything?"

"No. I'll be fine. I just need a nap. But thanks."

A half hour later, both my work and my body are done. All I want is to stretch out in the sun and let my bones melt. But first I have to put away my wagon and supplies.

As I cross the clearing to the wash-house, I catch the unmistakable drone of an airplane engine. That's odd, because this morning I heard Gabe tell Ed it was a plane-free day. I shield my eyes from the sun, waiting for the plane to come into view.

I'm not the only one who's heard it. Suddenly, people are heading to the dock from everywhere. Gabe is sprinting from his office. Ed is hurrying from the generator shed. The kitchen crew is traveling in a swarm from the lodge. Sid is trotting out from the trees. Dennis Savoy is even part of the parade, snapping pictures like the paparazzi.

I frown. I thought he was napping.

Something's not right. I abandon my wagon and follow the crowd. "What's going on?" I ask when I reach the dock.

It's Tricia, the kitchen girl, who answers me. "Meira burned her arm— bad. Dumped a pot of boiling water. Cook did what she could—soaked Meira's arm in lukewarm water and put plastic wrap around it. We gave her ibuprofen for the pain, too, but she needs a proper doctor."

As soon as the plane reaches the dock, Meira is helped aboard and Ed climbs in beside her. Gabe says something to the pilot, and then the plane is gone.

"All right, everybody, the excitement is over," Gabe tells us. "There will be an ambulance waiting for Meira in Kenora, and I'll let you know her condition as soon as I hear." He doesn't add, "Company dismissed," and no one salutes, but we all get the message.

The little knot of staff unties itself, and people return to what they'd been doing before. I start walking toward my wagon but stop when Gabe calls me and April. The two of us exchange puzzled looks and retrace our steps.

"I'm sure Meira is going to be fine," Gabe begins. "She has a bad burn, but Cook acted quickly, and that makes all the difference. However, she isn't going to be able to work for a while, which means we're short a waitress."

"I can handle things," April says. "I'll just speed up."

"I appreciate that, April," Gabe replies, "but we have to think of our guests. They pay good money for top service, and one waitress—no matter how hard she works—can't provide that service for a full dining room. You need help."

He turns to me. "I'm hoping that help is you, Bailey. I know you haven't done any serving before, but you're a quick learner." He pauses. "And April is a good teacher. Work as a team, and you girls can pull this thing out of the fire. Are you up for it?"

I don't know what to say. A few minutes ago I was dead tired, but the prospect of a new challenge has the adrenaline rushing through my body. I feel like I could run a marathon.

"I can try." I peer sideways at April. She looks stunned.

"April?" Gabe says.

She shakes herself out of her trance and nods. "Sure. Of course."

"Good." Gabe smiles. "There's one more thing. It's not fair to expect Bailey to serve in the dining room and clean cabins too, so until Meira gets back, I'd like you girls to share the duties. Bailey, you help April in the dining room, and April, you help Bailey with the cabins."

Chapter Six

"Poor Meira," I say as April and I enter the dining room for my crash course in waitressing. "What a horrible accident. Do you think she will be back?"

April lowers the water goblets she's checking for spots and blinks at me in disbelief. "Gabe said she would, didn't he? Meira might have burned her arm, but it isn't going to fall off. She'll be back.

She needs this job. Working up here might be fun and games for you, Bailey—a nice little cash bonus that you can blow on clothes, but the rest of us work to pay the rent and buy food. If we had other options, don't you think we'd take them?"

Whoa! Where did that come from? Outwardly I don't move a muscle, but inside I take a step back. This is obviously a sore spot with April.

"What are you talking about?" I frown. "I thought you were doing great. You said you were saving to open a flower shop. You told me you'd have enough this fall. But if you need to live on the money you earn here at the lodge, how is that possible?"

She doesn't answer. She just stares at me. Finally, she shakes her head. "Never mind." Then she motions to a stack of folded tablecloths. "Let's get these tables set."

Bang. The door on the subject is closed. For whatever reason, April is done talking about it. I don't push. But part of me can't help wondering if she ever really intended to open a flower shop. Maybe it was only a dream. After all, she never got past grade eight. If a university graduate has a hard time finding work, what chance does a high-school dropout have? If you have no job, how can you save for a dream?

The thought that I may have burst April's bubble makes me feel bad, but apologizing will probably make matters worse. So I grab an armful of linen and start on the tables.

A half hour before dinner, the guests descend on the lodge for appetizers and cocktails and to share stories about the day's fishing.

Since I'm underage, I can't serve alcohol, so it's my job to make sure the appetizer platters stay full and the empty glasses and plates are cleared. It's a good way to ease into dinner service. By the time the guests sit down to eat, my jitters are mostly gone, and I fall easily into the rhythm of things. First comes the salad, next the entrée and finally dessert and coffee. I keep an eye on April, trying to do what she does.

Dennis Savoy is at one of my tables. He's dining alone—unless you count his camera. I feel sorry for him. It can't be much fun to be on holiday by yourself. He doesn't seem to mind though. He's as smiley and chatty as ever. He's also hungry. He eats everything I put in front of him and even asks me to sneak him an extra dessert. But he's appreciative and leaves me a ten-dollar tip. Actually, all of my tables leave generous tips. No wonder April likes being a server.

After dinner, as April and I are setting the tables for the next day's breakfast, Gabe shows up.

"Good job tonight," he says quietly to me. "Thanks, Bailey." I see April watching us from across the dining room. I can't read the expression on her face, but when she realizes I see her, she looks away and goes back to work.

"What was that about?" she asks when we return to the kitchen.

As I unscrew the lids from the salt shakers, I say, "What was what about? Could you pass me that box of salt, please?"

She gives me the box and nods toward the dining room. "That thing with Gabe just now. What was he talking to you about?"

I shrug. "Nothing, really. He was just thanking me for helping out with dinner."

"Why didn't he speak to both of us?"

I look up in surprise. "I don't know. Maybe he wanted to reassure me, because he knew I was nervous." And then, realizing I've missed the shaker and dumped salt all over the table, I growl, "*Darn it!* Now look what you made me do." I grab a pinch of the spilled salt and toss it over my shoulder.

For once, April doesn't comment on my being superstitious. She's too amped about my conversation with Gabe. Her eyes narrow. "Are you sure Gabe wasn't promising you Meira's job *permanently*—or maybe mine? After all, he *is* your godfather."

I can't believe my ears. I stop cleaning up the mess and scowl at April. "What is your problem? Ever since Gabe said we'd be working together, you've changed. It's like you don't like me anymore. This isn't my fault. I didn't ask to be a waitress. I didn't ask for help with the cabins either. So get off my case."

April opens her mouth to yell something back, but then—almost magically—her face relaxes, and she shakes her head. "Sorry," she apologizes. "You're right. I don't know what's the matter with me. Maybe it's my hip. It's been killing me all day. And I have a major headache. I really need some sleep. Would you mind finishing up here? There's just the shore lunch boxes to do."

What am I supposed to say? I'm still ticked, but I don't want to be mean. "Fine," I mumble. Today April has been a regular Dr. Jekyll and Mr. Hyde. But I'm not looking for a war. I force a smile. "Sure. Go to bed. I'll take care of the shore lunch boxes."

Chapter Seven

Shore lunch is a fish feast prepared over an open fire by the guides. The lunch boxes are their portable pantries.

I check the list on the bulletin board against the contents I've placed inside. It's been a long day, and I can barely keep my eyes open. As for my brain, it's either already asleep or in a coma. The job takes way longer than it should.

When I'm finally sure the boxes are stocked down to the last potato and fork, I let myself out of the lodge and head for bed.

Right away, the fresh air chases away some of my drowsiness. I breathe it in hungrily and gaze up at the night sky. It's blue-black—dark, but not completely, so I don't bother switching on my flashlight. Though it's only about ten thirty, the camp is quiet. There are lights on in a couple of the cabins, including Dennis Savoy's, but the other guests have gone to bed. Out on the lake, a loon calls and a fish jumps. The gravel crunches under my feet.

I have the camp to myself—the camp and the moon. At one spot, the path opens to a clearing by the lake, and there it is—a huge white orb hung so low in the sky, it seems to sit on the water like an enormous pearl in a sea of diamonds.

As I marvel at the beauty of it, someone emerges from the trees. It's a girl. Right away, I sense an urgency about her. She moves quickly, but so fluidly that she seems to float. Her long hair and gauzy gown swing and sway with each step. She comes to a stop directly in front of the moon and reaches out to it—a black silhouette against glowing white.

Then, like a frantic hummingbird, she begins darting about the clearing—dropping, clawing the ground, springing up and moving on. Around and around she goes, becoming more and more frenzied with each pass.

It's the witch of the lake. I'm sure of it. The moon is full, and she's searching for her necklace.

I gasp and step backward—right into a bush. Leaves rustle and twigs snap. I drop my flashlight. The witch stops her feverish search and cocks her head to listen.

"Oh my god, oh my god, oh my god." I barely breathe the words, but I'm sure she's heard me. I clap a hand over my mouth.

She rises and takes a step toward me. She peers hard into the night.

I stop breathing. Is this really happening?

Silently I pray, *Don't let her see me.* I have no idea what would happen if she did, and I don't want to find out. I'm not one of the woodsmen who killed her mother, and I don't have her necklace, but maybe the witch doesn't care about that. I might be in trouble for disturbing her. I have no clue. This is my first encounter with a ghost.

After what feels like forever, the witch turns and lifts her arms to the moon again. Then she disappears into the trees.

That should make me feel better, but it actually makes me more scared. What if she's doubling back through the forest to sneak up behind me? There's no way I'm going deeper into the woods. I have to get back to the lodge.

I start to run. The crunch of the gravel beneath my feet is magnified by the quiet of the night, broadcasting my location like a loudspeaker. I might as well be wearing a flashing beacon on my head. If the witch wants me, I'm easy to find. But if I can get out of the woods, I'll be safe. At least, that's what I'm hoping. Every couple of seconds I look over my shoulder, expecting to see the witch closing in. Will she be herself or will she be a giant bear or a blistering fire?

I'm so concerned about what might be chasing me that I don't see what I'm racing toward—until I crash into it.

I'm swallowed by huge, powerful arms. I'm too stunned to scream, but my sense of survival takes over and I start punching and kicking like a crazy person.

My captor howls and lets go. My instincts tell me to run, but the path ahead is blocked by—

"Sloan?" I squeak as recognition sets in and relief washes over me. "Oh, man, am I glad to see you!"

"Oh yeah?" he growls. "You've got a funny way of showing it." He winces and rubs his side and then his shin. "Jeez, Bailey, what the heck were you tryin' to do? Kill me?"

"No. Of course not," I mumble. "Sorry." Suddenly, I feel really dumb. I peer over my shoulder again. "I thought you were…" I don't finish the sentence. If I tell Sloan I saw the witch, not only will he not believe me, but he'll laugh himself silly.

"You thought I was what?" he prods. "Voldemort? Dracula? Jack the Ripper?"

I shake my head.

"Then who?"

"The witch." I say it so quietly, it's a wonder he even hears me.

But he does. "The witch!" He snorts. "Are you kidding me?"

"Shhh," I hush him. "You'll wake the camp." Now my back is up. "Yes, the witch," I hiss. "I know you don't believe me, but I know what I saw. It was like Ed said. She was standing in the moonlight at the edge of the lake, looking for her necklace."

To my surprise, Sloan stops laughing. "Where?" he says.

I point down the path. "The clearing. But she's gone now. She heard me and slipped into the trees. That's why I was running. I thought she was coming after me."

I wait for Sloan to laugh again, but he doesn't. He's completely serious when he says, "Show me."

I can't say that I'm thrilled about going back to the scene of the crime, but at least I'm not going alone. If the witch wants to kill me, she's going to have to go through a big muscular guy to do it.

My flashlight is on the path where I dropped it. Sloan picks it up, flicks it on and starts wading through the long grass of the clearing. Against my better judgment, I follow.

At the lakeshore, he waves the beam of light over the sandy earth.

"Whewwwwww!" he whistles. "Somebody—or something—was here, all right. Look at this. The ground's all torn up and there are footprints. A girl's footprints."

I shake my head. "Not a girl. The witch."

"Come on," Sloan says, leading me back to the trail. "I'll walk you to your cabin."

We stop at the door. April has left the outside light on, and moths are fluttering around its hypnotic glow.

"Are you going to tell? You know, about the witch?" I ask. The last thing I need is to be the laughing stock of the camp.

He shrugs. "Not if you don't want me to. I saw the ground all torn up, but you're the one who saw the witch. It's up to you. If you want to tell, I'll back you up. If you don't, I won't say a word."

"Thanks." I point to the flashlight. "Take it. You can give it back to me tomorrow."

I quietly let myself into the cabin and shut off the outside light. I can hear April breathing softly in her sleep across the room. Should I tell her about the witch or shouldn't I? I have all night to decide.

Chapter Eight

I can't get the witch out of my head,
so it's a long time before I fall asleep.
When the alarm goes off, I'm not ready
to wake up. I look across at April's bed.
She's not in it. She's not in the bathroom
either. She must already have left for the
lodge. Since we usually walk together,
I'm sort of hurt.

I shower and hurry to the shed to get my little red wagon. It's not there. April must have taken it, but why? Gabe said she should help me clean cabins. He didn't say anything about delivering coffee. This is something April's decided on her own.

"Hey," I say when I see her loading up the wagon outside the kitchen, "I can do that."

She doesn't even look at me. "I got it. Cook could use a hand with breakfast prep though." Then, without another word, she starts for the guest cabins, and I have to jump out of the way to keep from getting run over.

"Morning, Cook," I say as I walk into the kitchen. "April said you could use some help."

Cook looks up from the ham she's slicing and scowls. "Are you responsible for the shore lunch boxes?"

I nod. "Yeah. Why? Is there a problem?"

Cook clucks her tongue and shakes her head. "You could say that. Three of them were messed up. No pork and beans in one. No flour in another. Another one was missing bread. You can't be making those kinds of mistakes, Bailey. It's a good thing April looked the boxes over this morning. If they'd gone out like you filled them, there'd be the devil to pay, and that's the truth."

"Really?" I say. "They were that bad? I checked each box twice against the list." I know I was tired when I was doing it, but did I really screw up *three* boxes?

Cook sighs and shakes her head. "I need some cheese grated."

I nod, but I have a rock in my stomach. This is not a good way to start the day.

It gets worse. As well as grating the cheese, I grate my finger, and Tricia has to take over. When April comes in, I'm in a corner buttering toast.

"The guides will be coming in for breakfast soon." Cook nods to the warming pans, so April and I start moving them into the staff dining room. I'm on my way back to the kitchen for another when there's a big bang.

"Bailey!" April hollers from the staff room.

I fly back. The floor is carpeted with scrambled eggs.

"What happened?"

She glares at me. "What do you think happened? You left the warming pan on the edge of the counter and it fell on the floor. Tell Cook we're going to need more eggs. Then help me clean up this mess."

I want to protest. I didn't leave the pan where it could topple over. Did I?

But now I'm not sure, and there's no time to argue, so I bite my tongue and do what April says.

The day is doomed. Before the guests show up for breakfast, Gabe cruises through the dining room and spots a dirty coffee cup on one of my tables.

"I know you don't wash the dishes, Bailey," he says, "but the tables are your responsibility. Imagine what a guest would think if he went to drink out of this."

It doesn't get any better. During service, an entire table has to ask for napkins. Another has no cutlery. How can I be screwing up so much? It's like my first week at the lodge all over again.

I'm actually relieved when it's time to clean cabins, especially when I find a four-leaf clover in the grass. I start at cabin one, and April starts with cabin eleven. She has the wagon, so I have to keep making trips back and forth to the washhouse to drop off soiled linen and get fresh stuff. It bugs me how April's taken over my job, but I don't say so. I don't want her to tell Gabe I'm complaining.

Finally, we're done, and we have some time to ourselves before dinner. I go back to where I saw the witch. The ground is still all chewed up. I'm relieved. It proves what I saw last night was real. I want to tell April, but she isn't exactly being friendly, so I decide to keep the witch to myself—for now, anyway.

As the fishing boats start returning, I head back up to the lodge. I pour myself a glass of lemonade and take it out to the back deck. Before I've had even a sip, Winnie comes storming out of the washhouse.

"What do you think you're doing?" she demands.

"What do you mean?" I look around guiltily, though I can't think what I could have done wrong. "I'm sitting down?"

"Not when there's work to be done, you're not," she says. "Guests in cabin three don't have any towels. You better be taking them some—right now—and make sure you apologize. Then you can take some toilet tissue to cabin four and say you're sorry to them too. Is this how you do your work? Sitting down? Because if it is, you can sit yourself down on the next plane out of here."

"Winnie, I'm…I'm sorry," I sputter. "Did I really forget to put towels and toilet tissue in the cabins?"

"Would I be telling you if you hadn't?" she hollers. "Don't ask silly questions. Just fix it! And when you're done, you can dust the lodge."

I deliver the towels and tissue and then head to the lodge with my duster. I'm in a fog. The day has been one disaster after another. It's bad enough that I'm screwing up, but I don't even realize I'm doing it.

The lodge doesn't seem to be the least bit dusty, but I give everything a thorough cleaning anyway. I don't want Winnie yelling at me again.

I work my way to Gabe's office. Maybe he'd like me to dust in there too. The door is open and I can hear a voice, so I don't knock. Instead, I take my duster to a table in the hallway.

I'm not really listening, but it soon becomes clear that the voice is talking on the phone. It's not Gabe. But that's not unusual. Cell phones are useless in the woods, so guests often use Gabe's phone.

I'm thinking I should probably come back later when I realize the voice belongs to Dennis Savoy. Suddenly, I'm curious.

"Yes, sir, that's right. I have all the information we need to proceed. I'll be leaving tomorrow as planned. I'll fax everything to you once I get back to my office."

My duster stops. What does that mean? It sounds like Dennis Savoy is at the lodge for business, not pleasure. But what business? He's a field investigator. I still don't know what that is.

I think about all the pictures Dennis Savoy has taken and all the questions he's asked me and other people at the lodge. Is he gathering evidence to use against the lodge somehow? Why would Savoy be investigating the lodge? Is somebody suing Gabe? Is the lodge involved in something illegal? Has Gabe broken some law?

Stop it! I scold myself. The man could be here for positive reasons. Maybe the lodge is up for an award. Or maybe the people Dennis Savoy works for are planning a big company trip.

I hear him say, "Absolutely. I'll be in touch as soon as I'm back in the city. Talk to you then. Goodbye."

Instant panic! If Dennis Savoy sees me, he'll know I was eavesdropping. But my run of bad luck is still holding. As I turn to leave, I knock an ornament off the table, and it clatters to the floor. I make a dive for it just as Dennis Savoy exits Gabe's office.

Sprawled on the floor at his feet, I look up and smile innocently. "Hi."

Chapter Nine

Dennis Savoy has to know I was eaves-dropping, but he just helps me to my feet and walks away. At dinner, he sits at one of April's tables. I'm glad. I would be uncomfortable serving him, especially since I can't decide if I should tell Gabe about his phone conversation. If the lodge is under investigation, Gabe should know.

On the other hand, I could get in big trouble for spying on a guest.

The next morning, the camp turns into a wilderness airport. From ten until noon, it's one plane after another, soaring off with our guests. Every last one of them. The weird part is that there are no more coming in.

When all of the guests have gone, Gabe calls a meeting on the dock.

"Okay, everyone. Listen up." He rubs his hands together thoughtfully. "We have an empty camp—though not for long. Tomorrow morning, we'll be bursting at the seams again. But today we can relax. So here's what I'm suggesting. Let's use the next few hours to prep for tomorrow's arrivals.

"After that"—his eyes start to twinkle—"we should unwind a little.

We've earned it." He smiles. "I suggest a little fishing derby, followed by a late shore lunch at George's lunch spot. What do you say?"

A mini cheer goes up.

Gabe glances at his watch. "All right then. Let's aim to be finished our work and back on the dock by four thirty."

I don't know who picked the teams for the derby, but I end up in a boat with April and Sloan. A few days ago that would have been great. But considering how cool April has been to me lately, I'm not exactly thrilled. Still, this is supposed to be a fun evening, so I paste a smile on my face and climb into the bow of the boat. April takes the middle seat, and Sloan, of course, sits in the stern.

He's totally straight-faced when he says, "Okay, girls, you better be ready to do some serious fishing, because I hate to lose."

April laughs. "Hey, you're the guide. You take us to the fish, and we'll reel them in." She turns in her seat and grins at me. "Right, Bailey?"

That catches me off guard. Lately, all April's done is scowl at me, so I'm not sure what to make of her smile. Is she saying she wants to be friends again? I guess time will tell.

I nod and smile back. "Absolutely."

We don't win the derby, but we do catch fish, and we have fun doing it. In fact, we laugh so much that by the time we get to George's lunch spot, my stomach hurts. April is back to her old self, and that is a huge relief. Taking on two jobs and having to train me was a lot of pressure. She was probably just stressed. I know I was.

"That walleye was so good!" Ed groans as he loosens his belt. "I wish I could eat it all over again."

"It was wonderful!" Cook exclaims. "I could use you fellas in my kitchen."

A few of the guides smile sheepishly.

"Well done, everyone," Gabe says. "But there's a ton of paperwork to do and somebody needs to man the phones, so I have to get back to the lodge."

Although I'm having a really good time, I think I should go back too. It'll give me a chance to tell Gabe about Dennis Savoy. I open my mouth to ask for a ride, but Winnie beats me to it.

She hauls herself up from the picnic table and says, "I'll come with you. I still have laundry to finish."

So much for that. I watch as Gabe and Winnie speed away, and then I help with the cleanup. Afterward, one of the guides pulls out a guitar, and everyone settles around the fire. Before you know it, we're singing up a storm. I notice April and Sloan are missing, but I don't think much of it. They probably want some time to themselves.

When Ed announces we're leaving in fifteen minutes, I head into the bush to get rid of the three cans of soda I've drunk. I'm not looking for company while I do my business, so I walk until I can barely hear the singing. Up ahead there's a monstrous rock. Perfect.

But as I undo my jeans, I hear voices. They're close, so I refasten my pants and listen. It's April and Sloan, and from the sound of it, they're on the other side of the rock. I start to tiptoe away, but when I hear my name, I stop.

"I have never seen anyone as superstitious as Bailey." April giggles. "Tricking her into thinking I was the witch was the easiest thing I've ever done! I wish I could've seen the look on her face. The way she took off, she could've won the Olympics. It was all I could do not to burst out laughing."

"You should've been in my shoes," Sloan says and snickers. "She ran into me like she'd been shot from a cannon. Then she started beating on me with everything she had. I've got major bruises."

"Aw, poor baby," April croons.

Suddenly it gets quiet, and I'm pretty sure I know what's happening. I should leave, but I'm too stunned to move. Although I heard April with my own ears, it takes a while for the truth of her words to sink in. There was no witch. It was just a mean trick.

April sneers, "The little princess has absolutely no clue. She's more trusting than a puppy."

"Why are you so hard on her?" Sloan says. "She's a kid."

"Yeah, a spoiled kid. The only reason Gabe took her on is 'cause she's his goddaughter. I worked as cabin girl for two whole summers before I got promoted to waitress. Bailey's here barely three weeks, and she gets moved up! She's used to being a guest—not staff. Working at the lodge is a game to her. She doesn't need the money."

"Maybe not like some people," Sloan concedes, "but you gotta admit she's a good worker."

"I don't have to admit anything," April growls. "Why are you sticking up for her?"

"Like I said, she's just a kid. The witch scam was one thing. It was funny, and I was okay with keeping Bailey occupied while you got back to the cabin. But you've really got it in for her."

"Are you referring to her little screwups yesterday?" April says. "That goes to show what a freakin' little innocent she is. No wonder her parents don't give her any freedom. She never suspected for a second that I was behind it. If anyone else messed up that bad, they would've got fired for sure, but not our Bailey." There's another pause and then, "Do you have any more beer?"

I feel my eyebrows shoot up. Alcohol is off-limits to staff.

"Not here. But back at camp. We can continue our party there—if you know what I mean." Sloan chuckles. "I'll bring the beer. You bring—"

Just then there's a shrill whistle, and my stomach does a flip.

"It must be time to leave," Sloan says. "Ditch these beer cans and let's get back before—"

I don't hang around to hear the rest.

Chapter Ten

I climb into the first boat heading back. As soon as it docks, I bolt for my cabin. I don't want to talk to anyone. I can take a joke, but what April did wasn't funny. It was mean.

I crawl into bed and stare at the ceiling. All I want is for sleep to come, but it's not even in the building. My eyes blur with tears that spill over and slide into my ears.

Angrily, I pound the bed. Why am I crying? Because I was tricked? Because I was the brunt of a joke? Because April doesn't like me?

It's none of those things. I've been pranked and laughed at lots of times, and April isn't the first person who hasn't liked me.

The thing that gets to me is that I trusted her. I opened up to her. I told her about myself—private stuff that I haven't shared with almost anyone. I thought she was my friend.

But she never was. She never liked me. She called me a princess. She told Sloan my secret, and she said I was spoiled.

Spoiled? *Ha!* At home, I have chores every single day, and I don't even get an allowance. I can really use the money I earn at the lodge.

But that's not the point. April's had it in for me from the start.

But why? It doesn't make any sense.

I'm still trying to figure it out a couple of hours later when April comes in. She doesn't turn on the light. Instead she stumbles around in the dark, bumping into furniture and then swearing like it was the furniture's fault. What she doesn't crash into she smacks with the plastic bag she's carrying. From the way it rustles and clanks, I'm guessing it's full of empty beer cans. Finally, April makes it to the bed and collapses. The bag of cans clatters to the floor.

I wake to early-morning sun and April snoring. The cabin reeks of stale beer. Since the new guests don't start arriving until ten o'clock, there's no rush to get up, except that I need some fresh air.

If I breathe in any more beer fumes, I'll be drunk too.

I shower and dress. April still hasn't moved. In fact, I don't think she's moved all night. She's sprawled facedown on the bed, fully dressed. There are beer cans spilling out of a plastic bag on the floor— a lot of them. I wouldn't be surprised if April stays passed out until tomorrow.

I think about getting Gabe. One look at April and she'd be leaving on the next plane. It's nothing less than she deserves, but—

A light goes on in my brain. Picking up my clock, I smile and set the alarm for right now. Then I stroll over to April's bed and pull the pin.

Instantly, the whole cabin starts jangling. I flinch, even though I know what's coming. April's eyes snap open and her body jerks off the bed. She grabs desperately at empty air, but it doesn't help, and she drops to the floor in a noisy heap, knocking the beer cans every which way.

"Oh god!" She belches and claps a hand over her mouth. Then she claws her way to her feet and stumbles to the bathroom, slamming the door behind her.

She's there for quite a while. When she returns, she has a wet facecloth pressed to her forehead. She looks like the walking dead.

"Headache?" I ask sweetly.

She glares at me. "Why did you do that?"

I frown. "Do what?"

"You know darn well what. The alarm clock."

I glance at the offending clock. "Oh, that. I guess I woke up early and forgot to turn it off. Sorry."

She lies down on the bed again and lays the cloth over her eyes.

"Are you sure you should do that?" I say.

"What?" she replies. Her voice is as lifeless as her body.

"Lie down. You might fall asleep again."

"That's the idea."

"Except that you might not wake up for a couple of days, and guests arrive in a couple of hours. It's going to take you at least that long to get ready."

April lifts the facecloth long enough to glower at me.

I sit down on my bed, and with the toe of my runner, I send a beer can rolling back to April's side of the room. "For starters, you need to get rid of these beer cans and air out the cabin—you know, in case somebody lights a match or in case Gabe comes in."

"Why would he?"

"Because he owns the place?" I clear my throat. "And you might want to think about having a shower and brushing your teeth. No offense, April, but you look like you spent the night in a garbage bin, and you smell like a brewery. Definitely not the image the camp is going for."

April props herself on an elbow and scowls. "You're enjoying this, aren't you?"

I cock my head curiously. "I'm just looking out for you." I smile brightly. "That's what friends do."

April starts to roll her eyes, but the effort obviously pains her because she gives it up and flops back down on the bed. "Go away," she mutters. "You're making me feel worse than I already do."

I stand up. "You know what you need? Food. You'll feel much better with something in your stomach. Some greasy bacon and fried eggs should do the trick, I think. Nothing like a little bacon grease to jumpstart the day. Before you know it, you'll feel like your old self. I bet you'll be up to pulling more tricks on me by lunchtime. Heck, you may even want to do your witch impersonation again." I stroll over to the door. "But then, that's not really an impersonation, is it?"

When April leaps off the bed, I think she's going to strangle me, but instead she bolts once more for the bathroom.

"See you at the lodge," I call after her and let myself out of the cabin.

As I start down the trail, I'm smiling. It feels good to give April a taste of her own medicine. But the feeling doesn't last. The two of us have to work and bunk together for another month, and that is not going to be easy. In fact, it could get downright ugly. I may have had a laugh at April's expense this morning, but if her claws come out all the way, I don't stand a chance.

As the trail opens into the clearing, I look around. The morning sun is dancing on the lodge windows and glistening in the dew on the lawn. Cellophane-winged dragonflies skim the surface of the lake in search of a mosquito breakfast. The camp is still asleep, except for me—and Gabe and Ed. They're standing on the dock, deep in conversation.

Suddenly I remember that I need to tell Gabe about Dennis Savoy's telephone call. What he'll make of it, I don't know, but I have to tell him. I should probably tell him about April too, but I won't. She may have broken a rule, but I'm not the lodge police. If she can do her job, it's none of my business. If she can't, Gabe will find out anyway.

I hurry toward the dock, but before I get there, Gabe takes off for the lodge. As usual, he's in a hurry.

"Gabe!" I call.

He looks up and waves but keeps on running.

"Can I talk to you?" I shout after him.

He turns and jogs backward. "Could we do it later, Bailey?" he says. "There's something I need to do that can't wait."

When I nod, he gives me another wave and resumes his run to the lodge.

Foiled again.

Chapter Eleven

Since I have nowhere else to go, I continue on to the dock. "Morning, Ed," I say with a sigh, staring at my feet as I drag myself along the boards.

He looks up from the rope he's coiling. "Aren't you a ray of sunshine," he says sarcastically. "Somebody pee in your cornflakes?"

I make a face. "No."

"Then why so glum?"

I sigh again. "I need to talk to Gabe, but he's always busy."

Ed goes back to coiling the rope. "That's camp life for you. Anything I can do?"

I think about that. Ed is Gabe's right-hand man, and no matter how busy Gabe is, he always has time for Ed. Maybe Ed could speak to Gabe for me.

"It's about a guest who just left— Dennis Savoy."

Ed chuckles. "The fisherman with no fishing gear."

"Right," I say. "The thing is, I accidentally overheard him on the phone in Gabe's office."

"Accidentally?"

"I was standing in the hall, waiting to go in and dust."

When Ed raises an eyebrow, I wince.

"I know. I should have left and come back, but I wasn't eavesdropping. Honest. I just have really good hearing."

"And?"

"Well, it sounded like he was talking to his boss. He said he'd gotten everything they needed to proceed. What do you think he meant? He's an investigator, you know."

"And you know this *how*?"

I lower my eyes. "I saw his business card. It was in the wastebasket in his cabin."

"You went through his trash?"

"Not on purpose," I say in my defense. "I knocked over his wastebasket, and I saw the card when I was cleaning up the mess."

"I see. So you think Dennis Savoy is investigating the lodge?"

"Yeah. Why else would he say those things on the phone? I mean, we know he isn't a fisherman, right? He admitted it. And he was always taking pictures and asking questions about the lodge and the staff and the work we do. Why would he do that if he wasn't investigating the lodge?" I pause. "Is the camp in some kind of trouble?"

Ed looks surprised. "Not to my knowledge. But if you like, I'll tell Gabe what you've told me."

Relief washes over me. "Thank you." Then I frown. "Do you think he'll be mad about me listening in on Dennis Savoy's phone call?"

Ed smiles. "I wouldn't worry about it." Then he changes the subject. "So where's your sidekick this morning?"

I tilt my head curiously. "Sidekick?"

"You know. April. I thought you two were inseparable."

I shrug. "Not really."

"Oh?"

"We kinda had an argument."

"Ah. Well, I wouldn't worry too much about that either."

"Why?"

He lays the coiled rope on the dock. "Things have a way of working out. Not always how you think they will or even how you want them to—but they work out."

The planes start arriving at ten sharp, and the camp goes from lazy to crazy. Because Drake and his trailer are needed to move supplies, the guides deliver the luggage. Gabe usually takes guests to the lodge to get their fishing licenses, but today he's needed on the dock, so April and I escort the new arrivals to their cabins. I'm coming as April's going, so we manage to avoid each other all morning.

It's a relief, but it can't last. Even if we could stay out of each other's way during the day, how are we supposed to manage at night? We share a cabin. We're going to have to talk sooner or later.

I think about the different ways it could go. We could freeze each other out. We could have yelling matches. We could continue to play dirty tricks on one another. We could have a knock-down, drag-'em-out fight. We could have a guarded truce. Or we could talk out our differences and start over.

I'd bet my entire summer wages that that last one's not going to happen— April isn't the forgive-and-forget type, and she was only pretending to like me in the first place.

The last guests arrive around eleven, and after showing them to their cabins, April and I head for the lodge to get ready for lunch service.

We're barely in the door when Cook says, "Gabe called from the dock. He wants you both back down there."

"What for?" April grouses. "Whatever he wants, the guides can handle it. We have to serve lunch."

Cook raises an eyebrow. "Since when do you call the shots around here? If Gabe wants you at the dock, I suggest you get your butts down there."

Sending Cook a snotty look and grumbling under her breath, April stomps back outside. I follow a good ten steps behind.

I shade my eyes and look toward the water. Another plane is taxiing in. I'm surprised. I didn't hear it coming. April's step quickens. She sees the plane too.

"More guests?" I hear her mutter.

Though I don't say anything, I don't see how that's possible. The camp is full. The plane must be carrying supplies. So why would Gabe want April and me to meet it? Drake's the delivery guy. All I can think is that maybe there's a cake or something else fragile that needs extra-careful handling.

"You wanted us, Gabe?" April says. She sounds totally pleasant. I'm amazed.

But Gabe and Ed are securing the plane, and he doesn't answer.

I try to see inside. It's a little four-seat Cessna. With the sun behind it, the interior is dark. I can't tell if there are passengers or not.

"This is ridiculous," April says quietly in my direction. They're the first words she's said to me since I woke her up. "We don't have time to be standing around here." She glances impatiently at her watch. "Guests are going to be coming in for lunch soon."

"Chill out, April," I say. "So lunch is five minutes late. It's not a big deal."

If looks could kill, I'd drop dead on the spot. "You've been doing this job a big three days. What do you know?" she snarls.

"What I know is that you don't handle a hangover well."

April takes a step toward me. "You little..." she growls through gritted teeth.

For a second, it's all I can do to stand my ground. April may be small, but she's tough. And then it all seems so stupid. "Oh, April, get over yourself," I say. "You're acting like a two-year-old. So you don't like me. Will beating me up change that? I thought you were mature and independent, but clearly I was wrong. I also thought you were my friend. Obviously, I was wrong about that too. But there's a lot of summer left, and we still have to work and bunk together, so suck it up."

To my surprise, April just stares at me.

I nod toward the plane. "Passengers are getting off."

Of course, the pilot is first. And right after him is—

"Meira!" April and I shout in unison, rushing forward to welcome her back.

Chapter Twelve

"Oh, Meira, it's so good to see you!"

"We've missed you."

"How are you feeling?"

"How's your arm?"

"Guys, guys!" Meira laughs, pushing through our hugs. "I've missed you too, but you're smothering me. I can't breathe. I'm good. The doctor says my arm is healing fine." She gently pats the bandage wrapped around her forearm. "Might not even have any scarring, thanks to Cook. I know it's only been a few days, but I've really missed the place. I can't wait to get to work."

"I can't wait either." April glares in my direction. "It's gonna be a relief to get back to normal."

Normal? And that's when it hits me—my time as a waitress is over. Now that Meira has returned, I'm the cabin girl again. Period. Although I never stopped cleaning cabins, the idea of going back to only that is deflating. Doing two jobs was a challenge, but it was fun waiting tables. Now the days are going to seem so long, especially since the friendship between April and me is over.

I know April's looking at me. I can feel her smugness.

"Good to have you back, Meira." Gabe smiles. "Can I assume the doctor has given you the all-clear?"

Meira nods. "Yup. I'm good to go."

"By the way, thank you for recruiting another staff member while you were in Winnipeg. I really appreciate it."

"No problem," Meira says. "It was good to have something to do." She turns back to the plane. "Come on out, Jen. Don't be shy."

A girl about my age climbs down from the Cessna.

"Everybody, this is Jen. Jen, this is April and Bailey—and Gabe, of course. He owns the lodge."

April and I mumble hello, and Gabe shakes Jen's hand. "Glad to have you aboard, Jen." Then he turns to April and me. "Ladies, Jen is going to be our new cabin girl."

"Cabin girl?" I say. I thought I was the cabin girl.

"There are *two* cabin girls now?" April says what I'm thinking.

"No." Gabe shakes his head. "Jen is taking over from Bailey. Bailey will continue working in the dining room."

I'm sure April's jaw hits the ground. I know mine does. "Bai—Bai—Bailey's going to keep waitressing?"

Gabe nods. "Yes."

"But—but why?" I can tell it's taking all of April's self-control to be reasonable. I bet she's screaming inside. If Gabe weren't there, she'd pounce on me like a feral cat. "Meira and I can handle the dining room," she continues. "We always have. It's not a problem. To tell you the truth, Gabe, I don't think there's enough work for three waitresses." April sends me a phony apologetic look.

"I agree," Gabe says.

"What?" April is clearly stunned.

"I said I agree with you. The lodge doesn't need three waitresses. That's why there are only going to be two."

April frowns. "I don't get it. You said Bailey is going to stay on as a waitress. That makes three—her, Meira and—"

A shuffling and bumping cuts April off, and we all turn back to the plane as a third passenger climbs out. It's a man. His face is hidden by a big brimmed hat, but once his feet are firmly on the dock, he lifts his head and smiles.

"Hello again, everyone."

It's Dennis Savoy.

He points to his head. "Made sure I brought a hat this time. Unfortunately, I won't be staying long enough to try it out on the water. Maybe next time. Right now, I need to talk to April."

"Me?" April exclaims. "Why do you need to talk to me?"

"It's a private matter," Dennis Savoy replies discreetly.

Gabe clears his throat. "Meira. Bailey. We need to get the new guests fed. So head up to the lodge. Take Jen with you and show her the staff dining room. Bailey, after lunch maybe you can help Jen get settled in." Then more quietly, "She'll be bunking with you."

I'm in shock. "What about April?"

"Something has come up. She won't be staying." Then Gabe turns to the pilot. "Come on, Jim. Let me buy you a coffee."

"Sounds good," Jim says. As he and Gabe head up to the lodge, Jim glances at his watch and calls to Dennis Savoy and April, "We'll be leaving in half an hour."

I feel like a tornado has blown through camp and turned everything upside down. My head is spinning, and my legs are wobbly. Halfway to the dining room, I look back at the dock. April has never looked smaller.

I serve lunch in a daze. I have no idea what's going on. Meira has no clue either.

If Cook knows something, she's not saying. Somewhere between soup and dessert, the plane takes off. Though no one has said so, I'm pretty sure April won't be back. Considering how she treated me, I should be doing a happy dance, but I actually feel a bit sad.

After lunch I take Jen to the cabin and tell her about camp life. I also promise to help her with cabins for a couple of days, until she gets comfortable with the routine. She seems nice. We could be friends, but I'm not going to rush into it this time.

In the middle of our conversation, there's a knock on the door. It's Gabe. I'm surprised. He's never come to the cabin before.

"I'd like to talk to you," he says.

I turn to Jen. "Make yourself at home. I'll be back."

Gabe doesn't waste any time. As soon as we step away from the cabin, he says, "Lodge staff come and go all season long, so no one needs to suspect April's departure is unusual. The official story is that she left for personal reasons—which is basically true. But because she was your cabin mate and because you knew something was going on with Dennis Savoy, I thought it only fair to tell you the whole story.

"Ed said you discovered Dennis Savoy is an investigator. You were one up on me. I didn't find that out until last night. However, he wasn't investigating the lodge—he was investigating April."

"April? Why?"

"I'm sure you know that April was in a motorcycle accident last year."

I nod. "The guy she was riding with died."

"And April was badly injured. So badly, in fact, that her doctor deemed her unable to work. Because of that, she was awarded a large insurance settlement."

I'm confused. "But April *was* working. Sometimes her hip hurt her, but it would always feel better after a night's sleep."

"That's the issue. The insurance company heard she was working here and sent Dennis Savoy to see if it was true."

"So now what?"

"April will have to appear at a hearing. If she can't justify the deception, she'll have to give the money back. She might also be fined. She could even go to jail."

"Are you serious?"

"Unfortunately, yes."

Things start to make sense. "What if she had a good reason for what she did?" I say.

"Like what?"

"Like trying to better herself. I think April was saving the insurance money to open a flower shop."

Gabe shakes his head. "It's good that she wants to improve her life, but she can't do it like that. That's part of April's problem. She plays by her own rules. She's got a chip on her shoulder. Sure, she's had a hard go of it, but so have a lot of people. That doesn't make it okay to abuse the rules and other people.

"This is April's third year at the camp. She's a good worker, but she has always had issues with people. As long as she's on top, she's sweet as pie, but if she's not, she can get nasty." He pauses. "But then, you already know that."

I blink at him in surprise.

He chuckles. "Not much happens at the lodge that I don't find out about, Bailey. I know about April's pranks on you. A little teasing can be fun, but she went too far. And, like I said, this wasn't the first time. That's why I let her go. Enough is enough. I only hope April learns a lesson from all this."

I'm numb. I don't know what to think. What April did was wrong, but I still feel sorry for her, especially when I think that I told Dennis Savoy about her plans to open a flower shop. Without meaning to, I contributed to her getting caught. I thought April had her life totally together. When I told Dennis Savoy about her, I was so proud. I wanted to be like her. Now I'm grateful that I'm not. My parents may be over-protective, but at least they look out for me. April has no one.

"Anyway, that's the long and short of it," Gabe says. "I'd appreciate it if you kept this to yourself." He squeezes my shoulder. "Keep up the good work. You're doing a great job. But don't forget to have some fun too. There's still a lot of summer left. Make it one to remember."

I sigh. "It already has been."

Cabin Girl is Kristin Butcher's fourth entry in the Orca Currents series. Her other Orca Currents titles are featured on recommended-reading lists such as the PSLA Top 40 (*Cheat*) and nominated for the YA Quick Picks list (*Caching In*). Kristin lives in Campbell River, British Columbia. For more information, visit www.kristinbutcher.com

orca currents

For more information on all the books
in the Orca Currents series, please visit
www.orcabook.com.